Simply The Power Of Prayer

D1564115

Copyright 2022

By: Pastor Angela Parkes

Used by permission.

Scriptures marked NIV are taken from the NEW INTERNATIONAL VERSION (NIV): Scripture taken from THE HOLY BIBLE, NEW INTERNATIONAL VERSION ®. Copyright© 1973, 1978, 1984, 2011 by Biblica, Inc.™. Used by permission of Zondervan

Scriptures marked NKJV are taken from the NEW KING JAMES VERSION (NKJV): Scripture taken from the NEW KING JAMES VERSION®. Copyright© 1982 by Thomas Nelson, Inc. Used by permission. All rights reserved.

DEDICATION

To my nephew Tyrone Curry 1988 to 2010

To my Mother Annie Curry 1954 to 2021

To my children Alexia Curry,

Ronnie Clemmons jr., Dequavius Curry.

To all my lovely grandchildren.

Special Thanks:

I would like to give special thanks to God the Father, Son and Holy Ghost. The late Hurley Coleman Sr. Mother Coleman, Apostle Edward Jackson, Co- Pastor Mattie Jackson, Bishop William Murphy Jr.,Prayer Partner Prophet Bobby Brandon, Evangelist Rita K. Boston, Prophetess Twinkle Jackson, Minister Aaron Jackson, and my friends and family for their prayers, encouragement and inspiration.

CHAPTER ONE- THE IMPORTATION OF PRAYER

I can remember as far back as nine years old when my grandfather and grandmother Pete and Annie Woods would take me to prayer meetings and shut-ins at the church. I grew up in Coleman Temple Church of God in Christ, in Saginaw, Michigan where the Pastor was Hurley Coleman Senior. My grandparents have since then gone on to be with the Lord. The Bible says, if you train up a child in the way he or she should go he would never depart and that is what my grandparents did with me.

"Train up a child in the way he should go: and when he is old, he will not depart from it". **(Proverbs 22:6 KJV)**

Growing up in my grandparents' home prayer never ceased. It was like clockwork. Every night before my grandparents went to sleep, they would watch the 11:00 news and then they would kneel on their knees and pray. Not at all understanding, at that time their impartation of prayer was being imparted unto me. I would always stay up until I heard them pray. They would call out their children's names and some of the children they would pray for longer and harder. Now that I have grown up, I understand why they prayed for some much longer and harder. Some of them were walking a different path than my grandparents had taught them. There was an impartation of prayer being imparted into me at that time that I had no knowledge of but God knew what he was doing.

When I was 13 years of age I no longer resided at my grandparents' home and as a result I quickly went astray from what they taught me. I got with the wrong children and eventually made all the wrong choices. I did everything I thought I was big and bad enough to do. There was no stopping me at that time.

I began to get in trouble, lots of trouble. I would call my grandmother and she would say pray and read the 23rd Psalms. Every time I found myself in some sort of trouble I would pray or call my grandparents to pray. Although I was getting into a lot of trouble I had been trained up in the way I should go. I had seen God move on the behalf of me and my family. As a child I felt the presence of God so I knew God was real and he could bring me out.

In 1998 things quickly begin to change. My grandfather became ill and on October 6, 1998, he passed away as a result of his illness. Meanwhile after his passing my grandmother was now separated from her husband whom she had been with for over 50 years. My grandmother began dating my grandfather at the age of 13 years old so you could imagine the bond they had formed. I became concerned about my grandmother and tried to stick close to her. She would still pray and trust God, but she really missed my grandfather. In 1999, which would have been exactly four months later, my grandmother suddenly passed away on February 6, 1999. I know my grandmother died of a broken heart. My grandparents carried our family in prayer. I knew someone was equipped and left with the mantle of prayer, but I never thought it would be me. I would hear my grandparents pray and ask God to save their children and their children's children.

"Keeping mercy for thousands, forgiving iniquity and transgression and sin, and that will by no means clear the guilty; visiting the iniquity of the fathers upon the children, and upon the children's children, unto the third and to the fourth generation. And Moses made haste, and bowed his head toward the earth, and worshipped. And he said, If now I have found grace in thy sight, O Lord, let my Lord, I pray thee, go among us; for it is a stiffnecked people; and pardon our iniquity and our sin, and take us for thine inheritance. And he said, Behold, I make a covenant: before all thy people I will do marvels, such as have not been done in all the earth, nor in any nation: and all the people among which thou art shall see the work of the LORD: for it is a terrible thing that I will do *with thee.*

(Exodus 34:7-10 KJV)

I know today that I am result of an answered prayer. After the passing of my grandparents, I began to go in and out of churches looking for a church home and a place where I could rededicate my life to Christ. I was looking to get back in right standing with God.

"And when he cometh home, he calleth together *his* friends and neighbours, saying unto them, Rejoice with me; for I have found my sheep which was lost." (**Luke 15:6 KJV**)

It took me until 2003 to find a place of rest where I could grow and be taught the Word of God. I had been in and out of churches. I would hang out all night long but on Sunday morning I would just pick a church. I would attend service sometimes never to return and some places I did return but did not join. There was a small church in Vassar, Michigan that my youngest sister was attending and invited me to visit. The pastor was Pastor Edward Jackson. In 2003 I joined the church and rededicated my life to Christ but I wasn't faithful yet. I would come here and there, but on May 22nd of 2004 it was like the day of Pentecost in that church. My hands and feet began to move uncontrollably it was just like fire shut up in my bones. I began to speak in an unknown tongue and I was filled with the Holy Ghost that day and from that day to this one I have not looked back.

"And when the day of Pentecost was fully come, they were all with one accord in one place. And suddenly there came a sound from heaven as of a rushing mighty wind, and it filled all the house where they were sitting. And there appeared unto them cloven tongues like as of fire, and it sat upon each of them. And they were all filled with the Holy Ghost, and began to speak with other tongues, as the Spirit gave them utterance." **(Acts 2:4 KJV)**

In 2006 the church purchased another church in Saginaw, Michigan. As we were approaching the move to the new church home, we had a church meeting. We wanted to set the new church in order and the pastor who is now an Apostle, posed a question. He wanted to know who would like to be over seer of intercessory prayer. I immediately raised my hand but some of the members felt I wasn't qualified. They silently murmured. Many didn't come because they felt it should have been someone who was more seasoned in the faith than me. That did not stop the call on my life to intercede for God's people. We had prayer every Thursday faithfully and God would send the people. Some members were faithful to prayer and some would come out when they were going through trials and tribulations. Some members came whenever they felt like it but God would always have people who would pray. I remained faithful being the intercessory prayer leader for Christ Kingdom Ministries until August of 2015. In August of 2015 God called me into full time ministry to pastor a church of my own. I never even dreamed I would be pastoring but God had a plan for my life. To God be all the Glory! This book was inspired by God. I pray your prayer life through Christ Jesus and this book will be enriched forever.

CHAPTER TWO- WHAT IS PRAYER?

What is prayer?

1. Prayer is a way in which we contact the Father
2. We talk to him and tell him what's on our minds
3. We tell God what we have need for
4. We tell God what we're going through
5. Prayer is telling the Lord how much we love him
6. We let the Lord know our appreciation
7. It's also our opportunity to let God know how grateful we are to him.

There is no other way to contact God but by prayer. Prayer is a conversation between God and man, but it's also two-way communication. Prayer is a way of communication for all denominations. This is the one expression to God that has not been argued. In other words all denominations realize the need to take it to the Lord in prayer. Prayer, when it is done in Faith and in sincerity results in answers from God.

Prayer is communion with God. Prayer is a spiritual expression that brings us into conversation with God. Prayer is how our relationship with God begins. When we first ask the Lord to come into our life we pray and ask him to come in. This is the beginning of our communing with God, when we ask our Father to come into our heart and save us. Prayer will also cause God's will and purpose for your life to be fulfilled.

Every good relationship starts with good communication. When there is very little communication or none at all relationships suffer.

Good Communication is:

1. Sharing your thoughts and ideas,
2. Problems
3. Ups and downs in your life
4. Sharing the things that are important to you with someone you believe understands and can help you.

Prayer is communication with God. Telling him everything that is on your heart. We must take our burdens to the Lord and the only way to do that is to communicate with God, which is prayer. Prayer is also giving God thanks for all he has done for us. Just as all other relationships in our life require communication so does our relationship with God.

Prayer is a way of connecting to God so that he may give you instructions. The same way you would connect to another person via or by way of the telephone is the same way you would connect to God via or by way of prayer. Prayer is a straight line to God the Father himself. No longer does the priest have to go in for us the veil has been rent that we may pray for ourselves. The way to God is now open we now have direct access to him

"And, behold, the veil of the temple was rent in twain from the top to the bottom; and the earth did quake, and the rocks rent;"
(Matthew 27:51 KJV)

"Jesus, when he had cried again with a loud voice, yielded up the ghost. And, behold, the veil of the temple was rent in twain from the top to the bottom; and the earth did quake, and the rocks rent; and the graves were opened; and many bodies of the saints which slept arose, and came out of the graves after his resurrection, and went into the holy city, and appeared unto many. Now when the centurion, and they that were with him, watching Jesus, saw the earthquake, and those things that were done, they feared greatly, saying, truly this was the Son of God. **(Matthew 27:50 -54 KJV)**

Prayer forms a relationship between the Father and the child, the Creator and the creature, the Master and the servant, the Supernatural and the natural, the Divine and the human. It is through prayer that God gives instruction. We must listen for his instructions, and it is through prayer that God gives direction. Prayer is what causes things to come to pass in your life. It is also through prayer that we get to know God for who he really is. Just like the heart needs oxygen and the body needs food so does the Spirit man need prayer.

Prayer is way for a man to make his request known unto God. When he has made his request known unto God, God being the eternal Father that he is in turn answers the man. Therefore the answers will cause the man to begin to get an understanding and at that time he also begins to come unto the knowledge of the truth, that God is the one true and only living God. Now the only way to know this is to form an intimate relationship with God through prayer.

God's people never outgrow the need for prayer. Christianity is built on prayer; you may be thinking to yourself how that is if Jesus is our foundation. Jesus is our foundation and he said in his word no man comes unto the Father but through me, there is no other way to get to him but by prayer. We go to God in prayer using the name of Jesus. A dentist pulls teeth, a doctor prescribes medicine, and a Christian prays.

Prayer is what I found myself doing when I was taken from my mother. **Prayer** is what I was doing when I didn't have a father in my life. **Prayer** is what I was doing when I became pregnant at the age of 16. **Prayer** was what I was doing when five of my family members were killed in a fire. **Prayer** is what I was doing when I found myself alone with two children at the age of 19. **Prayer** was what I was doing when I was shot at. **Prayer** was what I was doing when I got in trouble with the law. **Prayer** was what I was doing when my great-grandmother passed away. **Prayer** is what I was doing when my grandfather passed away. **Prayer** was what I was doing when my grandmother passed away. **Prayer** was what I was doing when my cousins and friends I grew up with passed away. **Prayer** is what I found myself doing when my family gave up on me. **Prayer** is what I found myself doing when my children went astray. **Prayer** is what I found myself doing when I was wounded by church folks. **Prayer** is why I am where I am in life today.

In 2021 when I found myself in a place where I lost a dear friend and an assistant in the ministry. A powerful woman of God. She gained her wings and exactly one week later I lost my mother. God had given me my mother for 50 years of my life. She loved me unconditionally. My mother always encouraged and gave me words of wisdom when I needed them. She always knew the right thing to say to me. A part of me had left with her. It felt as if a ton of bricks was placed on my chest and my arm would fall off. I didn't know what to do but it was prayer that got me through.

The following week I lost my Godbrother whom I loved dearly. We were more like brother and sister, not having the same parents is what separated us from being biological siblings. Blood couldn't have made us closer. I was hurt, on top of hurt, on top of hurt. Not only that, one month later after being married for 13 years I found myself facing a divorce. I was being faced with all these drastic, heartbreaking, and disappointing things in my life. I could have lost my mind. I could have given up but it was Simply the Power of Prayer that kept me. I am still here today preaching, teaching, exhorting, lifting, and comforting God's people. God did not let me fall he kept me! Again, it was Simply The Power of Prayer.

CHAPTER THREE- HOW TO BEGIN?

When we read the word of God, which is the Holy Bible. Jesus gave us an example of how to pray he said after this manner pray. Manner is the way in which something is done or happens.

"After this manner pray ye: Our father which art in heaven, Hallowed be thy name. This is how we show our love and adoration for God and a way of petitioning the father. We are giving him reverence. We are also acknowledging he's Holy Thy kingdoms come. Thy will be done in earth, as it is in heaven. We are praying for the reign of God which would be complete when there is a new heaven and a new earth. And his will to be done instead of ours. Give us this day our daily bread. We are acknowledging God as our daily provider and petitioning God for what we need daily. And forgive us our debts, as we forgive our debtors. We are asking God to forgive us for our sins and in turn we are going to forgive those who sinned against us. And lead us not into temptation, but deliver us from evil: For thine is the kingdom and the power and the glory, Amen." **(Matthew 6: 9-13 KJV)**

We are asking God to guide us so that we don't fall in to temptation, and at the end of this prayer we are giving God praise for who he is!

When we begin prayer it is important that we acknowledge God for who he is to us. This is an act of giving him reverence. I always begin with heavenly Father. I've heard some people use the term "kind" Father, or some just simply say "Father", but whatever works for you as long as you reverence God as your Father. When Jesus walked the earth, he always reverenced his Father. Jesus was our example and what an awesome example he was.
*The first step in praying is always having a repentant and forgiving heart.

Scripture says in **Matthew 6:14-15 (KJV)** For if ye forgive men their trespasses, your heavenly Father will also forgive you: But if ye forgive not men their trespasses, neither will your Father forgive your trespasses.

We begin prayer in sincerity and faith, believing that God will answer our prayer. In order to enter into his courts we must enter in with praise and thanksgiving. We also must come humbly and boldly before the Throne of Grace.

The word of God tells us that the prayers of the righteous man availeth much.

"Confess *your* faults one to another, and pray one for another, that ye may be healed. The effectual fervent prayer of a righteous man availeth much" **(James 5: 16 KJV)**

You may not have been in church all your life and you don't understand the term a "righteous man," but nevertheless you can be a righteous man or woman. A righteous man or woman is simply one who abstains from sin. He or she doesn't want any part of sin. He or she turns from sin never to return. If at any time they fall they quickly get up. A righteous man does not practice sin, although he's not perfect he or she wants no part of sin.

*__Prayer__ must come from the heart and be different every time. Prayer is not something you rehearse. If it's rehearsed there is no sincerity in it and it's not from the heart at all. If it comes from the heart, you're more adamant and serious about what you are praying. You also become more likely to pray to God until the prayer is answered. This is because its burning in your heart and you become passionate about it. The reason the prayer should be different every time is because we will always have a different request or concern. We may not understand something and have to ask God for understanding. There may even be times when we just pray to God by giving him thanks and telling him how much we appreciate him. Sometimes our prayer may be on our knees and then there are other times when we could be standing or even laying prostrate. The prayer you pray for your child will be different from the prayer you pray for your neighbor. Although you love your neighbor there is a bond you carry with your child that you will never have with your neighbor or any family member.

There will also be a difference in praying for a saved and unsaved person. You should always pray God would draw them by his spirit. You can pray for their health and mind. Ask God to make them strong where they are weak. Spiritual and natural growth is always good to pray for because everyone needs it in their daily walk with Christ. God said in his word no man comes unless he draws them. The most important thing we can pray for an unsaved person is for salvation. Salvation should be at the top of the list for them. On the other hand, a saved person you would be praying for God to give them strength in their walk with Christ. You would pray that because the enemy which is the devil continues to set traps for them to make them fall until they leave this world. Satan lost his place in heaven, so he doesn't want any of the saints to make it in. These are just some examples of the reason prayer would be different in some instances.

It is very important that you be real with God. Whatever you do, don't try to mimic anyone else's prayer because they sound good. No matter how good they sound if it is not sincere and coming from the heart it's all in vain. Praying like someone else can't be sincere because you're not being you. Remember what Jesus said about the person that wanted to be heard for there much saying:

Matthew 6:9 says, "But when ye pray, use not vain repetitions, as the heathen do: for they think that shall be heard for their much speaking."

God is Omniscience, this means he is all knowing so therefore God knows when we're being real. Our Father knows the very number of hairs that are upon our head. God made us wonderfully and uniquely, so we don't need to mimic anyone else.

CHAPTER FOUR- WHY SHOULD WE PRAY?

In order to form a relationship with God we must pray. In forming this relationship, we become closer to God. How can we get to know God if we don't pray? We need to spend time with God in prayer because it develops are relationship with God in a more intimate way. It is in prayer where we learn his voice. God is only a prayer away and he has a listening ear.

Why pray? Prayer is where God reveals his plans for your life to you. God does this by giving instruction and direction. God will send a prophet, prophetess, a man or woman of God, and sometimes even a mere stranger to reveal his plans to you. If you've been in prayer, it will only confirm what God has already told you. Instead of you being shocked by what you're hearing, it would come as confirmation to you. If we pray, we can also avoid the snares and traps of the enemy. God will be able to warn us beforehand if we're spending time with him in prayer. Prayer gives us the power to resist temptation. The Bible tells us to, "Watch and pray, lest you enter into temptation." **(Matthew 26:41)**. We need to pray so that we have the strength to avoid sin in other words. If we don't spend time in prayer we become weak. However, the enemy knows this, and he fights prayer but if we continue in prayer we gain strength and power and are less likely to become weak.

*Jesus gave us instructions to pray in **Luke (18:1),** and he spake a parable unto them to this end, that men ought to always pray and not faint.

Jesus was our example and he consulted the Father in prayer consistently and if Jesus did it so should we. Although Jesus had to go through situations on this earth nothing happened that he was not already aware of. It is in prayer that we get our strength from God.

If Jesus had not gone to God in prayer, he might not have had strength to take the fact that one of his own disciples betrayed him. Jesus may have not had the strength to be nailed on the cross for our sins.

We should pray because it causes the things that God wants to do here on earth to be manifested. If we pray in faith and sincerity it results in answers. We also pray that we may here from God. Prayer causes us to gain spiritual growth; we need prayer in order to grow in Christ. When we pray God gives us a lay out of instructions to help us on our journey with him.

EXAMPLE:
We get up in the morning praying and thanking God for another day. If we tell God how much we love him, and then we get a phone call from a person that has offended us. They call crying and are in desperate need and want us to do something for them. Our flesh says the way they did me! I know they are not calling me. Since we have been praying, THE SPIRIT OF THE LIVING

GOD speaks to us and tells us immediately you will not render evil for evil. If we obey, we will grow in the Lord and in our walk with him. If we are not praying it's hard to hear and get to know him. Not hearing him can render this evil. It will hinder our walk with Christ and this evil is what causes us to fall. We can get up, but we have to start over because we haven't been in prayer.

When you have a test, you have to prepare for it by studying. Along the same lines, when you want to walk with God you pray so you can get to know him. How can we know someone whom we have not talked to? How can we know God's voice if we don't pray and let him give us answers, direction, instructions, and guidance. It is through all of this that we get to know him. We get all of this through prayer.

When we are not praying this is what happens:

1.) We keep falling because we have no direction. We start to feel like were going in circles looking for answers to our problems, we just know we need answers. We need answers in our homes, jobs, churches, schools, marriages, families and so on. The good news is the answer is only a prayer away. How can we get the answer unless we pray?

Prayer unleashes God's power so he is able to work on our behalf. Prayer also opens the channels of God's blessings. Prayer is how God accomplishes the things that he wants to see happen in our lives, and in the lives of others. Prayer opens new doors of opportunity for God to move in.

We should pray because the Lord instructed us to pray. One of the simplest reasons to spend time in prayer is because the Lord taught us to pray. Obedience to God is a must in our walk with Christ.

CHAPTER FIVE- HOW OFTEN SHOULD WE PRAY?

Prayer should take place morning, noon, evening, and night. In the morning when we get up we should arise giving God thanks for another day and for keeping us all night long.

"Very early in the morning, while it was still dark, Jesus got up, left the house and went off to a solitary place, where he prayed."
(Mark 1:35 NIV)

When you start your day off with prayer It blesses your entire day. The word of God tells us:

"It is of the Lord's mercies that we are not consumed, because his compassions fail not. They are new every morning: great is thy faithfulness." (**Lamentations 3:22-23 KJV)**

In the afternoon we should continue to give thanks to the Lord.

"O give thanks unto the Lord; for he is good: because his mercy endureth forever.
(Psalm 118 KJV)

When we give God thanks it's just like one would be with their own child. When a parent knows a child appreciates them it compels them to do more, the same way with God. When we have an attitude of gratitude towards God, he in turn blesses us. Throughout the day we should also be asking God to order our steps right.

In the evening we should continue giving God thanks. If there is no other prayer you pray, we should always pray the prayer of thanks

"In everything give thanks: for this is the will ofGod in Christ Jesus concerning you."
(1 Thessalonians 5:18 KJV)

When night fall we should pray before we go to bed. We should pray for ourselves, families, neighbors, and those in authority. We should also pray for whatever and whoever else God lays on your heart to pray for.

In 2005 shortly after I had gotten saved, I was experiencing some difficulties. My utilities were shut off in my home. I got saved and I made up my mind that I was going to live for Christ. The illegal activities that I was doing before I gave my life to Christ to get gain, I decided at that time I was no longer going to do. As a result of not doing those illegal activities anymore to get gain I found myself with no money and no way to pay my bills. I had a full-time job at that time but my checks were being garnished so each week that I worked my check was zero dollars and zero cents. As a result, my utilities was shut off I had to remain in the dark for a while but during that time I didn't give up on God. I would light a candle and read my Bible. On this particular night I lit a candle and I was reading my Bible and praying and while I was reading and praying I fell asleep. During the time when I fell asleep I left the candle lit without any knowledge and not being aware that I had left this candle on. I woke up the next morning to get ready for work and found the candle had burned out. I had a small chair the candle was sitting on and a decorative chair that set on my dresser. The candle burned the wood on that chair and it burned a letter that was on my dresser. The fire went out and nothing else burned. The dresser didn't burn I mean the fire just completely went out the entire candle burned up! God spared my life! I believe because I prayed, read my Bible, and talked to God that night he kept me. That's why we should pray before we go to bed

You should pray until something happens. Whenever we are about to eat we should thank God for our food and ask him to bless it. The Bible tells us that we should pray without ceasing Thessalonians 5:17 ("Pray without ceasing") that means we don't ever stop praying. We should pray in our cars, for ourselves, and the other drivers that are on the road with us. In the doctor's office we should pray for a good report.

The Bible also says that men are to always pray.

"And he spake a parable unto them, to this end, that men ought always to pray, and not to faint," **(Luke 18:1 KJV)**

Those were the instructions given by Jesus and if we follow his instructions we can't go wrong. This means that at all times we should be praying and while we're praying we should not get tired. However, at times the answer to our prayer can take longer than we would like it to, but we cannot give up we have to trust God. Knowing that God is able to do exceedingly abundantly above all we could ask or think.

The only time we shouldn't pray is to be seen of men.

"and when you pray, you shall not be as the hypocrites are: for they love to pray standing in the synagogues and in the corners of the streets, that they may be seen of men. Verily I say unto you, they have their reward." (**Matthew 6:5**)

We want our reward from God so we shouldn't pray so others can see how good we pray or how spiritual we are. If we do that, we get our reward from people and not from God. I don't know about you, but I want my reward from God. Everything we do should be unto God, this is a sure ticket to Heaven.

We should pray at all times because Prayer Changes Things. Prayer stops the devil in his tracks. Praying is a way you can cover yourself with the blood of Jesus. You can escape things through prayer. We don't know it but sometimes after we pray there's some unseen things that were coming our way and God stopped those things before those things were even able to get to us.

We should pray consistently as shown in the scripture found in (Acts 1:14, NIV) They all joined together constantly in prayer, along with the women and Mary the mother of Jesus, and with his brothers. When you want to be refreshed revived and renewed it is sometime necessary to pray all night long.

"Now it came to pass in those days that He went out to the mountain to pray, and continued all night in prayer to God. " **(Luke 6:12, NKJV)**

When we continue in prayer any request we make will be granted.

"But if you stay joined to me and my words remain in you, you may ask any request you like, and it will be granted!" **(John 15:7, NLT)**

"Then Jesus told his disciples a <u>parable</u> to show them that they should always pray and not give up." **(Luke 18:1, NIV)**

"And pray in the Spirit on all occasions with all kinds of prayers and requests. With this in mind, be alert and always keep on praying for all the saints." **(Ephesians 6:18, NIV)**

What If I Don't Know How to Pray?

The <u>Holy Spirit</u> will help you in prayer when you don't know <u>how to pray</u>

"In the same way, the Spirit helps us in our weakness. We do not know what we ought to pray for, but the Spirit himself intercedes for us with groans that words cannot express. And he who searches our hearts knows the mind of the Spirit, because the Spirit intercedes for the saints in accordance with God's will."
(Romans 8:26-27, NIV)

Are There Requirements for Successful Prayer?

The Bible establishes a few requirements for successful prayer:

- A humble heart

"If my people, who are called by my name, will humble themselves and pray and seek my face and turn from their wicked ways, then will I hear from heaven and will forgive their sin and will heal their land." **(2 Chronicles 7:14, NIV)**

- Wholeheartedness

"You will seek me and find me when you seek me with all your heart." **(Jeremiah 29:13, NIV)**

- Faith

"Therefore I tell you, whatever you ask for in prayer, believe that you have received it, and it will be yours." **(Mark 11:24, NIV)**

- Righteousness

"Therefore confess your sins to each other and pray for each other so that you may be healed. The prayer of a righteous man is powerful and effective." **(James 5:16, NIV)**

- Obedience

"And we will receive whatever we request because we obey him and do the things that please him." **(1 John 3:22, NLT)**

Does God Hear and Answer Prayer?

God hears and answers our prayers. Here are examples from the Bible.

"The righteous cry out, and the LORD hears them; he delivers them from all their troubles." **(Psalm 34:17, NIV)**

"He will call upon me, and I will answer him; I will be with him in trouble, I will deliver him and honor him." **(Psalm 91:15, NIV)**

See Also:

- 1 Samuel 1:27

- Psalm 4:3

- Psalm 18:6

- Proverbs 15:29

- Isaiah 58:9

- Luke 11:9

Why Are Some Prayers Not Answered?

Sometimes our prayers are not answered. The Bible gives several reasons or causes for failure in prayer:

- Disobedience - Deuteronomy 1:45; 1 Samuel 14:37

- Secret Sin - Psalm 66:18

- Indifference - Proverbs 1:28

- Neglect of mercy - Proverbs 21:13

- Despising the Law - Proverbs 28:9

- Bloodguiltiness - Isaiah 1:15

- Iniquity - Isaiah 59:2; Micah 3:4

- Stubbornness - Zechariah 7:13

- Instability or Doubt - James 1:6-7

- Self-indulgence - James 4:3

Sometimes our prayers are refused. Prayer must be in accord with God's divine will:

"This is the confidence we have in approaching God: that if we ask anything according to his will, he hears us." **(1 John 5:14, NIV)**

(See also - Deuteronomy 3:26; Ezekiel 20:3)

"Very early in the morning, while it was still dark, Jesus got up, left the house and went off to a solitary place, where he prayed."
(Mark 1:35, NIV)

"Yet the news about him spread all the more, so that crowds of people came to hear him and to be healed of their sicknesses. But Jesus often withdrew to lonely places and prayed." **(Luke 5:15-16, NIV)**

"Now it came to pass in those days that He went out to the mountain to pray, and continued all night in prayer to God." **(Luke 6:12, NKJV)**

CHAPTER SIX- TYPES OF PRAYER

Corporate prayer is when a congregation comes together and pray. Corporate prayer could also be several congregations coming together. God wants us to pray together with other believers. There is power when we all get together in prayer. The Bible says one can chase a thousand two can chase ten thousand so the more we come together and pray the more power we have.**(Deuteronomy 32:30)**

The Prayer of agreement is a type of prayer. There is also power in agreement prayer. It's good to have someone who believes as you do to agree with you in Jesus' name and it shall be done. Scripture says in, **(Matthew 18:19, NIV)** Again, I tell you that if two of you on earth agree about anything you ask for, it will be done for you by my Father in heaven.

There are scriptures in the Bible that show us where the people of God Prayed together, for example in **(Luke 1:10, NIV)** And when the time for the burning of incense came, all the assembled worshipers were praying outside.

"They all joined together constantly in prayer, along with the women and <u>Mary the mother of Jesus</u>, and with his brothers." **(Acts 1:14, NIV)**

God also wants us to pray alone and in secret place with just us and him the Bible says in **(Matthew 6:6, NIV)**

"But when you pray, go into your room, close the door and pray to your Father, who is unseen. Then you're Father, who sees what is done in secret, will reward you."

"Very early in the morning, while it was still dark, Jesus got up, left the house and went off to a solitary place, where he prayed."
(Mark 1:35, NIV)

"Yet the news about him spread all the more, so that crowds of people came to hear him and to be healed of their sicknesses. But Jesus often withdrew to lonely places and prayed."
(Luke 5:15-16, NIV)

There is no correct or certain posture for prayer. In the Bible people prayed on their knees (1 Kings 8:54), bowing (Exodus 4:31), on their faces before God (2 Chronicles 20:18; Matthew 26:39), and standing (1 Kings 8:22). You may pray with your eyes opened or closed, quietly or out loud— however you are most comfortable and least distracted. God created everyone different. There is not one of us that have the same fingerprint, that is how strategic God was when he was creating us. We are fearfully and wonderfully made. (Psalms 139:14)

Personally, I mostly walk the floor and pray. The majority of the time I don't even realize it but I would be just talking to God sharing my feelings or concerns about myself or someone else. Then I would end up in prayer crying out to God on behalf of myself or others the majority of the times it's for others. When we cry out to God he hears us. Scripture says this, The righteous cry out, and the LORD hears them; he delivers them from all their troubles. **(Psalm 34:17, NIV)**

 There are times when I am compelled to fall on my knees, however there are other times when I'm prostrate on my face. It seems this is the time when God really speaks to me. There are many types but you must find the place where you're most comfortable.

CHAPTER SEVEN- POWER IN PRAYER

In chapter 5 I discussed how the Lord brought me through the night when my candle burned my dresser and chair. God spared my life! I know my life was spared that time as a result of prayer. That's one of the reasons we should pray because I am a living testimony that God saved my life through prayer. I could have burned and been found in that fire but God put that fire out and I thank God for that. Why pray you ask? In 2007 I was experiencing chest pains. My chest was hurting unbearably, and I began to pray and pray and pray. One day I was in the congregation in the midst of people where the pastor was praying. He said there's someone in this audience experiencing chest pains and whoever you are God is going to heal you. At that moment I stood he prayed for me and later on I realized that I was no longer having chest pains. We ask, why pray? In prayer miracles happen, deliverance happens, salvation happens, and healing takes place. That's why we pray.

Around 2014 my son got in trouble and was facing 20 years in prison for a foolish mistake he had made involving his girlfriend. At the time he was charged with breaking and entering into a home that he was living in. I prayed and I prayed and I prayed and as a result he was able to walk away free with only probation and, we ask why I pray.

In 2012 my daughter's home was shot up with her fiance at the time, her two children, a three year old, and a two month old in the home. The entire home was shot up from top to bottom and she and my two grand babies survived. I know without question that God spared her life and my two grandchildren lives.

CHAPTER EIGHT-PREPARING YOURSELF TO PRAY

The very first and foremost thing is we must have a repenting heart before God. Whenever we come before God we want to have a clean heart and a right spirit.

If we want to release successful prayers the Bible gives us instructions. We must have a humble heart and turn from sin. To repent means to stop and turn away from. There are steps we must take when we come before God. We don't want our prayers to hit the ceiling we want them to reach our Father.

"If my people, who are called by my name, will humble themselves and pray and seek my face and turn from their wicked ways, then will I hear from heaven and will forgive their sin and will heal their land." **(2 Chronicles 7:14, NIV)**

- When we seek the Lord we must seek him wholeheartedly. God doesn't want part of us he wants all of us and if you give him all you will never regret it. The songwriter says "He Wants It All"

"You will seek me and find me when you seek me with all your heart." **(Jeremiah 29:13, NIV)**

If we don't have Faith when we go to the Lord in prayer there is no sense in praying. If we don't believe he can do it why are we praying? If we would only believe God can move mountains in our lives and do great and mighty things. But we have to trust God and have faith in God.

"Therefore I tell you, whatever you ask for in prayer, believe that you have received it, and it will be yours." **(Mark 11:24, NIV)**

- Righteousness

"Therefore confess your sins to each other and pray for each other so that you may be healed. The prayer of a righteous man is powerful and effective." **(James 5:16, NIV)**

- Obedience

- *"and we will receive whatever we request because we obey him and do the things that please him."* **(1 John 3:22, NLT)**

CHAPTER NINE- PRAYING THE WORD OF GOD

"For the word of God is quick, and powerful, and sharper than any two-edged sword, piercing even to the dividing asunder of soul and spirit, and of the joints and marrow, and is a discerner of the thoughts and intents of the heart"
(Hebrews 4:12 KJV)

God has given us the Word of God as a weapon and as a tool. The Word of God is no good to us if we do not use it as the weapon it is. Whenever the enemy comes against you and you use the Word of God, the enemy will have to flee.

The Word of God is sharper than any two-edged sword. That means the Word of God won't miss but you must pray the Word and use it. The Word of God helps you separate the soul and the spirit. It also separates the joints and marrow. The Word goes deep down inside and it does not miss.

Praying the Word of God

Praying the Word of God is using Scriptures as you pray and using God's Word in your prayer.

When you pray the Word of God it causes your prayers to be effective. When we say God's Word and put it in the atmosphere, we are saying his Word back to him. Whatever God sets his Word to do it accomplishes it. When we use God's Word in prayer it accomplishes whatever we are praying for.

I pray the Word of God based on different situations and circumstances.

1. Healing- If I'm praying for healing, I would speak by your stripes they are healed in Jesus' name. (Isaiah 53:5)
2. Finances/In need-If someone is in need I would decree and declare, that their cup shall run over. (Psalm 23)
3. Job- If someone is looking for a job or a door to be opened I would pray knock and the door will be opened (Matthew 7:7-8)

Beginning to Pray the Word

You might ask, how do I pray the Word of God. The first thing you must do is read and learn the Word. You can't pray the Word if you don't know his Word. When you read and learn the Word what goes in will come out. Reading and studying the Word causes the Word to take root and ground your spirit. Once the Word is rooted and grounded in your spirit, while you are praying the Holy Spirit will bring the Word to your remembrance. The Holy Spirit will bring the Word for you to pray for the very person, situation, or circumstances you are praying for.

If you are new or you don't know where to start praying the Word, I recommend reading the book of Psalm. Spending time in Psalm sharpens your prayer life.

Here are some foundational Scripture passages that you can read in Psalm:

1. Psalm 23

2. Psalm 27
3. Psalm 37
4. Psalm 91

Prayer Partner

It's good to pray by ourselves and it's also good to have a prayer partner. If you are new to praying, it's important to partner with someone who is experienced in prayer. What happened for me was when I first got saved I connected with an older woman. I called her one day and said that I was getting ready to go on the highway to Chicago. She prayed for me and the prayer she prayed ignited something in me. It was like a prayer mantle came on me after that prayer.

If you don't have a prayer partner the more, you pray the more the Holy Spirit gives you. The more you pray the more understanding he gives you. The more you pray the more your eyes are opened and you begin to be more enlightened. When you pray you can see your prayers being answered and things opening up for you. Prayer starts a relationship with God. Having a relationship with God allows things to open up to you. Prayer causes you to get a revelation and a deeper understanding of things that you are praying for. There may be a position that you want and through prayer you see doors open. You get knowledge, revelation, and understanding through prayer. Prayer makes you look at things from a different perspective. Instead of seeing things from a negative side you will see things from a positive perspective. For example, there may have been an incident and you had to go to the hospital. Instead thinking negative because you are in the hospital. Since you've been praying and have a relationship with God, you thank him to getting to the hospital in time.

Mature Christians

I've discussed where someone can start if they are new to the faith and to reading the Word of God, but I also want to challenge those that are seasoned.

If you are a seasoned Christian, I would recommend reading Ezra 5. Ezra 5 is a passage that can get overlooked. It is a good passage of Scripture about prayer.

Testimonies of Praying the Word of God

My mom had an infection on her kidneys and they ended up removing her kidneys. My mom coded a couple times. The doctors asked us if we should let her go or bring her back. They said if we brought her back that she would only be able to function at 10%. I stood on the Word of God and by his stripes she was healed. It wasn't just me but my family prayed with me that by his stripes she was healed. They brought her back and she lived three more years. She was a lot higher than 10% too. She was around 85%. My mom walked, talked, and did what she wanted to do.

I encountered a young man that was facing jail time. I told him to pray Psalm 56. He prayed that Scripture every day and as a result he didn't do any jail time. He reads Psalm 56 to this day. He's doing well and has his own business now.

We should pray the Word of God regularly because his Word activates his power.

CHAPTER 10- INTERCESSORY PRAYER

Starting Intercessory Prayer

You can begin intercessory prayer by developing a prayer life. Praying morning, afternoon, evening, and at night will help you develop your prayer life.

There is a difference between a prayer warrior and an intercessor. A prayer warrior fights while an intercessor feels.

When you intercede for someone, you empathize and feel what that person feels. God will take you to a place where you feel exactly how that person feels. He will allow you to put yourself in that person's position. An intercessor will feel the person's hurt, pain, and disappointment when they are praying for them.

The Holy Spirit will give you who you should intercede for. You may not know them personally, but the Lord can put them in your spirit to intercede. The Lord has entrusted you to intercede for them.

The Holy Spirit works in different ways. Sometimes when he gives you a person to intercede for, he may not tell you anything about them. If he doesn't tell you about them it's not for you to know, it's for you to PRAY. You can pray for God to help them in whatever they need. They may need healing, deliverance, or a financial blessing, whatever it is you can intercede. The Holy Spirit can also give you a person with the specific thing that person is going through. If God gives you someone to intercede for it should be kept between you and God.

The gift that God gives intercessors is to feel what they feel and pray what needs to be prayed. Intercessors' prayers are so empathic it can seem like they are praying for themselves.

Getting stronger as an Intercessor

An intercessor can get stronger by:

1. Being led by the Holy Spirit
2. Continuing to PRAY

3. Continuing to read the Word of God, specifically Psalm.

People tell me they believe God has called them to intercede for others. They tell me they can feel what the person is feeling and it seems like they are with that person when they are praying. When people come to me believing they are called to intercede, I tell them to begin reading the book of Psalm. I tell them to lay and stay in the book of Psalm because it helps you develop your prayer life.

How God has used me in Intercessory Prayer

There was a guy battling an alcohol addiction and God was using me to intercede for him. I could see him in front of a bottle and him going to resist it. God was giving me the power to intercede for this man to have the strength to resist and say no to alcohol. As the result of God using me to intercede for him, he was delivered from alcohol addiction.

I was the leader of the Intercessory Prayer Ministry at the church that I attended in Vassar. We had 12 Hour Prayers and Shut-ins, where we interceded for others. We took topics that people were going through that year and interceded for them. Topics like marriage, singleness, finances, etc. were distributed to intercessors to pray. As the lead intercessor I personally knew the intercessors and the topics they were zealous about. I also allowed the Holy Spirit to lead me on what topics to give the intercessors to pray for.

The topic or area that burdens an intercessor the most is the area they should intercede for. My passion are souls. I intercede for souls to be saved. Lost souls are what burdens me the most. If you have a zeal for marriage or a zeal for people who lack, those will be the people you would intercede for.

12 Hour Prayer and Shut-in Prayer

The 12 Hour Prayer and intercession is just what it says we intercede on different topics for 12 hours.

The Shut-in Prayer is when the intercessors intercede on different topics, read the Word, and have praise and worship all night long. Before we have our Shut-in, we do a 10 day Daniel Fast. During the 10 days we are praying together and meeting to preparing for the Shut-in. The intercessory team are the ones that are in attendance at the Shut-in.

The results of 12 Hour Prayers and Shut-ins:

1. People become closer to God and desire more. They desire to be closer to God, used by God, live a lifestyle for God, they learn to pray and intercede for others
2. Individuals become stronger in God
3. Gifts are stirred up
4. Causes people to want to live for Christ
5. Salvation takes place
6. Deliverance takes place
7. People are healed

I've seen people come in the Shut-In with one leg higher than the other and they left walking straight. Some people have come in the Shut-In on a cane and left without the cane. There have been people to come in with pain in their body and leave pain FREE.

One young lady came to the Shut-In and by the Holy Spirit she was taken back to the time when she was a little girl. She was brought back to her childhood when her uncle molested her. She was hunted, depressed, couldn't rest, and she had a lot of walls up. Walls of hurt, shame, and disappointment were up. Through this prayer she came up and testified about how she felt so FREE. The young lady said that she had FORGIVEN her uncle and was ready to move on with her life.

There was a person that came to the Shut-In that was in a same sex relationship. After the Shut-In they testified they were done with that lifestyle. They said they felt a cleansing while they were in the Shut-In. They were ready to move on and allow God to bring someone into their life.

There was a young lady that came to the Shut-In that was suicidal. She had a plan to take her life. She had attempted a couple times before she came to prayer. After the Shut-In she testified that she did NOT want to take her life any longer.

CHAPTER 11- PRAYERS

UNITY PRAYER

Heavenly Father we come to thee, thanking you for another day, another year, and another breath. Father we thank you that you are King of kings and Lord of lords beside thee there is no God. You are the Alpha and Omega, Beginning and the End. Father God we pray that you would have your way on today. Father we pray that this would be the beginning of the Body of Christ coming together as a whole on one accord, not just the local church but all churches whether they are big or small. We bind up division in the body of Christ in the name of Jesus we loose oneness and **Unity** in the Holy Ghost. We pray that you would bless us all to speak the same thing and that we be perfectly joined together in one mind and the same judgment in Jesus' Name Amen....

"Now I beseech you, brethren, by the name of our Lord Jesus Christ, that ye all speak the same thing, and [that] there be no divisions among

you; but [that] ye be perfectly joined together in the same mind and in the same judgment.
(1 Corinthians 1:10 KJV)

Prayer for Singles

Heavenly Father I thank and praise you for what you have already done in my life. For with you all things are possible but without you nothing is possible. Father as I put you first, and build a personal relationship with you, I pray that you would hear my voice and know that it is my desire to have a Spirit filled mate. In Jesus' Name Amen.

Order My Steps

Heavenly Father as I begin to take this new journey this year, I ask that you would order my steps in your Word and in your way. I pray that I will walk in the calling and purpose you have for my life. Most of all I pray that your perfect will be done in my life. Father God this year belongs to you. In Jesus' Name Amen.

Order my steps in thy word: and let not any iniquity have dominion over me.
(Psalms 119: 133 KJV)

Desires of my Heart

Father I put you first and build a personal relationship with you. I pray that you would hear my voice and know that it is my desire for you to build Godly relationships for me. Whether it be marriage, fiancé, family, church family, or just a simple friendship. In Jesus' name Amen.

"Delight thyself also in the Lord; and he shall give thee the desires of thine heart."
(Psalms 37:4 KJV)

Launching into the Deep

Heavenly Father I pray that you would give me a deeper understanding of you. Father bless me that I might leave the shallow and launch out into the deep. Take me beyond the natural and into the supernatural. I decree and declare a deeper revelation of you, a deeper **Knowledge**, and **Wisdom** to my fullest **Capacity.** In Jesus' name Amen.

"Oh Lord, how great are thy works! And thy thoughts are very deep" **(Psalms 92:5 KJV**)

Bearing Good Fruit

Heavenly Father I ask that you would rain down your Holy Spirit upon me and bless me to be free from sin, that there would be increase in my life, both spiritually and naturally. Bless me to bear all the Fruits of the Spirit. The fruit of love, joy, peace, long suffering, gentleness, goodness, faith, meekness, and temperance. In Jesus' name Amen.

"Then will I give you rain in due season, and the land shall yield her increase, and the trees of the field shall yield their fruit." **(Leviticus 26:4 KJV)**

Spiritual Growth

Heavenly Father I ask that you would pour out your spirit that I may blossom and grow into the man or woman you have called me to be. It is my desire to read your Word and to know your Word that I may grow and mature in you Father, that I might be that example for you and Glorify you Father. Lord I want to be planted like a tree by the rivers of living water. In Jesus' Name Amen.

"As newborn babes, desire the sincere milk of the word that you may grow thereby."
(1 Peter 2:2 KJV)

Being a light for God

Heavenly Father, I come to you now asking you to bless me and be glorified in my life. I pray that my light would out shine darkness day in and day out. Lord I ask that Salvation, Deliverance, and the Holy Ghost would shine through me that people would feel your presence when I'm among them and want to know about you and begin to say, what must I do to be saved. In Jesus' name Amen.

"Let your light so shine before men, that they may see your good works and glorify your father which is in Heaven." **(Matthew 5:16 KJV)**

Repentance

Heavenly Father I come to you with a repenting heart, repenting for every thought, word, or deed that was unlike you. Oh, Father that the Holy Ghost would fall upon me like never before. Lord that the fire of God rest upon me and never go out. Father I need your Holy Ghost Power Morning, Noon and Night. In Jesus' name Amen.

"I indeed baptize you with water unto repentance: but he that cometh after me is mightier than I, whose shoes I am not worthy to bear: He shall baptize you with the Holy Ghost and with fire." **(Matthew 3:11 KJV)**

Increase

Heavenly Father I come to you now seeking and asking for **increase**. Father I pray for increase in every area of my life **Spiritually, Emotionally, Physically,** and **Financially** and Father I thank you in advance for the **Increas**e. Father most of all I ask that you would bless me to **increase** and abound in the Greatest Commandment of all which is **LOVE**. In Jesus name Amen.

"And the Lord make you to increase and abound in love one toward another, and toward all men, even as we do toward you."
(1 Thessalonians 3:12 KJV)

Binding and Loosing

Heavenly Father I thank you that you have given us power and Authority over the enemy, and I break the curse of satan off of my life and off of my family's life. I lift up the fatherless, the widows, and the orphans unto you. I bind up a sinful nature, unforgiveness, illness, disease, and poverty and in its place I **loose** Salvation, forgiveness, health, long life and prosperity. In Jesus' Name Amen.

"Verily I say unto you that that whatsoever will be bound earth should be bound in heaven." **(Matthew 18:18 KJV)**

Promotion

Heavenly Father I pray for promotion in the Spirit realm as well as the natural. Father I ask that you would bless me to be successful in life, and that everything I touch would turn to gold. Most of all Father I pray that I would decrease and you would increase in my life, more of you Father and less of me. You get the glory in everything I do. In Jesus' name Amen.

"For promotion cometh neither from the east, nor from the west, nor from the south. 7: But God is the judge: he putteth down one, and setteth up another." **(Psalms 75: 6-7 KJV**)

Favor

Heavenly Father I thank you for the precious blood of Jesus. I thank you for my life, my health, and my strength. I thank you for Salvation and the Holy Ghost. Thank you for all that you have done for me and how you have kept me over the years. I thank you and I give you praise. I pray that the **favor** of God would rest upon me all the days of my appointed time. Father I ask that you bless my going and my coming with the **favor** of God always. In Jesus' name Amen.

"And the Angel said unto her, fear not, Mary: for thou has found favor with God." **(Luke 1:30 KJV)**

Eternal Life

Heavenly Father I thank you for sending your Son Jesus to die on the cross for my sins. I thank you for the precious Blood of Jesus. Father I love you and I adore you. I call your name wonderful; I call your name Mighty God, The everlasting Father, The Prince of Peace, Most High God, Emmanuel God with us. In Jesus' name Amen.

"For unto us a son is given: and his name shall be called wonderful, Counselor, The mighty God, The Everlasting Father, The Prince of Peace." **(Isaiah 9:6 KJV)**

PRAYER FOR YOUR CITY

Heavenly Father I thank and praise you for what you have already done in this City. For with you all things are possible but without you nothing is possible. Father as we put you first and build a personal relationship with you. We pray that you would hear our voice and know that it is our desire to have a Spirit filled and Peaceable **City.**

We come against Violence in this **City** and we loose Peace on every street, block by block and street by street. Satan we take Authority over you right now in the name of Jesus, We decree and declare peace from the North, South, East and West side of town. We command Violence to stop in this **City** now. We plead the blood of Jesus Christ of Nazareth over this entire **City.** We take back our **City** by force. We pray for the families that have lost loved ones through Violence. Father we ask that you would comfort their hearts and minds. Father we also pray for Justice for every family in the name of Jesus. We cry out in these streets for peace, a peace that passes all understanding. For we walk by faith and not by sight believing that there shall be peace in this **City** and we thank you Father that it is so in Jesus name AMEN! "Peacemakers who sow in peace reap a harvest of righteousness."

"And the fruit of righteousness is sown in peace of them that make peace." **(James 3:18 KJV)**

Marriage

Heavenly Father we thank you for marriage. For we know that marriage is ordained of you and we ask Father God that you would cover our marriages in your blood, that you will protect our marriages from the plot and snares of the enemy. We decree and declare that what God has joined together no man will pull asunder and Father we asked that you would turn the husband's heart to his wife and the wife's heart to her husband and both their hearts to you. We thank you Father that they shall be married until death do them part in Jesus' name amen.

"So they are no longer two, but one flesh. Therefore what God has joined together, let no one separate." (**Matthew 19:6 NIV**)

Illness

Heavenly Father I come to you thanking you for what you have already done and asking you for a healing Father. I ask that you would heal my body from the crown of my head to the soles of my feet. Your word says by your Son Jesus' stripes we are healed. I know you are a healer Father God and I receive your healing unto myself right now in Jesus' name Amen.

"But he was wounded for our transgressions, he was bruised for our iniquities: the chastisement of our peace was upon him; and with his stripes we are healed." **(Isaiah 53:5 KJV)**

Family

Heavenly Father,

I come to you as humble as I know how, asking you to save my family and to bless them. Knit our hearts together so that we may be the family that you have called us to be. We bind the devil that would come and try to separate our family in the name of Jesus. We plead the blood of Jesus Christ of Nazareth over our family. We decree and declare that no weapon formed against our family shall prosper in Jesus name Amen!

"No weapon that is formed against thee shall prosper; and every tongue that shall rise against thee in judgment thou shalt condemn. This is the heritage of the servants of the Lord, and their

righteousness is of me, saith the Lord."
(Isaiah 54:17 KJV)

Health

Heavenly Father I place my health in your hands and I stand on your Word. Your Word says Beloved I wish above all things that thou mayest prosper and be in good health even as thy soul prospers. I decree and declare over my life that I am Healthy, Wealthy, Well, and made whole in Jesus' name!

"Beloved, I wish above all things that thou mayest prosper and be in health, even as thy soul prospereth." **(3 John 1:2 KJV)**

Crisis

Heavenly Father, I thank you that even in the midst of adversity you're still God and you're in control. You reign and rule over everything, you are able to do exceedingly abundantly above all we could ask or think! So, Father I thank that you are bringing me out of this Crisis and you're bringing me out with Victory. I release my faith and I give everything to you in Jesus' name!

"Now unto him that is able to do exceeding abundantly above all that we ask or think, according to the power that worketh in us, Unto him be glory in the church by Christ Jesus throughout all ages, world without end. Amen." **(Ephesians 3:20-21 KJV)**

Depression

Heavenly Father, I pray that you would cover my mind in your blood. Father God make me strong where I'm weak. Father give me beauty for ashes, the Spirit of Joy for mourning, and a garment of Praise for the Spirit of heaviness. Father you get the Glory out of my life. Lord give peace that passes all understanding. When I'm in trouble I go to the Rock, the Rock that is higher than I. I bind depression and I loose Peace thank you Father for being my Rock! In Jesus' name I pray Amen.

"Fear thou not; for I am with thee: be not dismayed; for I am thy God: I will strengthen thee; yea, I will help thee; yea, I will uphold thee with the right hand of my righteousness." **(Isaiah 41:10 KJV)**

Police Officers

Heavenly Fathers whose great powers and eternal wisdom embraces the universe watch over the police officer. Protect them from harm in the performance of their duties to stop crime, robbery, riots, and violence. We pray that you would help them and law enforcement keep our streets and homes safe day and night. We commend them to your loving care because their duty is dangerous. Grant them unending strength and courage in their daily assignments. Dear God Protect them and grant them your almighty protection. Unite them safely with their family after duty has ended in Jesus' name Amen!

Closing

Sometimes it's for you to pray and sometimes for you to say. For example, God can give you a person to pray for. He may give you specific details to pray. The Lord may tell you to pray for a person's health, financial situation, or the person's family. Sometimes the Lord will give you those details **JUST** to **PRAY**. Meaning the Lord doesn't want you to tell that person you are praying for them he just wants you to pray.

On the other hand sometimes God will direct you to tell the person what the Lord revealed to you about them. This allows the person to be aware of what the Lord is saying concerning that person. It also lets them know that they are on your mind and you are praying for them.

When we believe God works, when we listen God speaks, and when we pray God listens. As a result the hand of God will divinely intervene and change takes place in our lives.

Remember prayer is communion with the Lord. Prayer is a spiritual expression that brings us into conversation with our Lord God. Prayer is how our relationship with Jesus Christ begins.

62211855R00046